Kevin Thinks

...about Outer Space, Confusing Expressions and
the Perfectly Logical World of Asperger Syndrome

Gail Watts

Jessica Kingsley *Publishers*
London and Philadelphia

We wish to acknowledge the Ballarat Saints Basketball Club, the Buningyong Football Club and the Australian Football League for their kind support.

First published in 2012
by Jessica Kingsley Publishers
116 Pentonville Road
London N1 9JB, UK
and
400 Market Street, Suite 400
Philadelphia, PA 19106, USA

www.jkp.com

Library of Congress Cataloging in Publication Data
A CIP catalog record for this book is available from the Library of Congress

British Library Cataloguing in Publication Data
A CIP catalogue record for this book is available from the British Library

ISBN 978 1 84905 292 4
eISBN 978 0 85700 615 8

Printed and bound in China

For Reilly

This is Kevin.

Kevin thinks you should always do up the top button.

Why else is it there?

Kevin thinks he might not finish his dinner.

He is worried about what the food might do to him.

Kevin thinks Mum is ridiculous saying that he is wasting the sunshine and fresh air.

As if it would ever run out!

Kevin thinks his yellow cap is the best.

Lots of kids at school really like it.

Kevin thinks the new football jumper
Grandma gave him is annoying.

Every time he wears it,
perfect strangers are mean to him.

Kevin thinks that you should be able to do whatever you like on your birthday.

After all, it is *your* day.

Kevin thinks kids should not get upset if they lose points for being late for tennis.

Those are the rules.

Kevin thinks that he is not very good at dancing.

Nobody ever wants to be his partner.

Kevin thinks it is unfair that he is always last to leave school, because Mum is always messing about with something.

Kevin thinks his 'computer brain' is awesome because he can remember lots and lots of important facts about outer space, computers and football players.

Kevin thinks 'outer space' is really interesting.
He tries to talk to the kids at school about
outer space, but they are not really interested.

Mum loves outer space. She can listen for hours
and always tells Kevin how clever he is.

Kevin thinks it is annoying when people touch his things,

especially when he has worked so
hard to put them in order.

Kevin thinks the new clothes that Mum has bought him are scratchy and uncomfortable.

He is much happier in his old clothes.

Kevin thinks you should always tell the truth.

No matter what, always tell the truth.

Kevin thinks that eyebrows are confusing.
When Dad's eyebrows are up it means Dad is happy.
When Dad's eyebrows are down it means Dad is cross.

But what does it mean when Dad
raises just one eyebrow?

Kevin thinks it is weird that Mum always wants to watch movies that make her cry.

Why would anyone want to be so unhappy?

Kevin thinks his Aunty Blue is a bit silly at times.

He wonders why a grown up person
would behave that way.

Kevin thinks that shopping centres are
too bright, too noisy and boring

— but he can always find something to do there.

Kevin always worries that he will say
or do the wrong thing and upset people.
He feels like he is always in trouble.

Sometimes Kevin gets confused and very, very angry.

Kevin thinks he is lucky to have Mum and Dad to help him learn all the rules about people. One day he will remember them all and he will be all right.

But sometimes Kevin thinks...

...he would just like to be alone.

So, who really cares what Kevin thinks?

Well, many people famous for changing the world sometimes think how Kevin thinks. They have been successful because they think in a different way to other people.

They have been able to think of amazing things that no one else had thought of.

So, maybe one day the whole world
will be interested in
what Kevin thinks.

Author's Note

I remember the day my son was diagnosed with Asperger Syndrome. I came home from the doctor's and tried to make a cup of tea, but I could not hold on to the kettle for all my shaking and bawling. I am not quite sure why I was so upset, I did not even really know what Asperger Syndrome was. 'It's on the autism spectrum,' the doctor said, but my son was not like the children I knew who were autistic. So I set out on a quest of self-education. All I had was the internet, a library card and an unstoppable drive to understand. Eventually, I came to the conclusion that it was a relief to have this diagnosis. Finally we had explanations for my son's odd behaviour and strategies to help him. Raising this boy has been hard work, but also a joy and a privilege. My son is 16 years old now, and is growing into a fine young man who I am enormously proud of.

This book started out as sketches and scribblings to record, for myself, my son's stories. I often jotted down funny things my children said or did in a little journal. This book is filled with true life stories, as I remember them, of the social difficulties that my son encountered when he was a little boy.

Through the character, Kevin, this book shows us many traits that are common in children who have a diagnosis of Asperger Syndrome. For instance, Kevin has an inability and lack of desire to interact with his peers and is also unable to interpret or appreciate social cues, facial expressions or tones in people's voices. Kevin often displays socially and emotionally inappropriate behaviour and he does not understand how anything he does affects other people. Many people with Asperger's have a 'special' interest and Kevin loves 'outer space' – to the exclusion of everything else! Kevin also has sensory sensitivity to light, noise and scratchy clothes. Kevin takes everything that is said to him literally and does not understand sarcasm or when people are only teasing.

This book gives us an insight into the world from the perspective of a child with Asperger's. The written text tells us what Kevin is thinking, but we need to look at the illustrations to see what is really happening. His thoughts tell us his logic and explain his sometimes inappropriate behaviour.

I hope this book will be used by parents to explain Asperger Syndrome to siblings, family and friends of children with Asperger's. Every page could be used by parents or teachers as a stimulus for discussions on social situations. This book highlights many social conventions that could provide teaching material for lessons on values, tolerance and bullying.

Lastly, this book carries important messages about tolerance and understanding of children who may think and behave in a different way to their peers. It tells children that it is okay to be different, because of the wonderful things that you might have to offer the world one day.

If you think about it, perhaps there is a little bit of Kevin in us all.

Gail Watts

of related interest

Frog's Breathtaking Speech
How Children (and Frogs) Can Use the Breath to
Deal with Anxiety, Anger and Tension
Michael Chissick
ISBN 978 1 84819 091 7
eISBN 978 0 85701 074 2

The Red Beast
Controlling Anger in Children with Asperger's Syndrome
K.I. Al-Ghani
ISBN 978 1 84310 943 3
eISBN 978 1 84642 848 7

Can I Tell You About Asperger Syndrome?
A Guide for Friends and Family
Jude Welton
ISBN 978 1 84310 206 9
eISBN 978 1 84642 422 9